SO-DJW-753

CONTENTS

Meditation   **Page**

1. Beginning at Lod 7
2. A Roman Capital 11
3. Mount Carmel 13
4. Nazareth 15
5. Wedding at Cana 19
6. The Sermon on the Mount 21
7. Capernaum 25
8. On the Shore 29
9. The Country of the Gadarenes . . . 31
10. The River Jordan 35
11. Zion 37
12. Two Upper Rooms 39
13. Mount of Scandal 41
14. The Old City 43
15. The Golden Gate 45
16. Gethsemane 49
17. The Pavement 53
18. The Place of a Skull 57
19. The Tomb 61
20. Mount Olivet 65

21. The Hill Country 67

22. Road to Bethlehem 69

23. Silver Star 71

24. Shepherds' Field 75

25. Down to Jericho 77

26. House of God 81

27. Mizpeh 83

28. Wealth in Samaria 85

29. City of Refuge 87

30. View from Pisgah 91

Preface

This is the logbook of a journey in the Holy Land. It suggests readings from the Bible for each day, with descriptions of the places and thoughts that arise therefrom.

Everybody cannot go to see the land where Jesus lived and where the events of the Old Testament took place. Flying may make such a journey easy, and tours are remarkably cheap and well arranged, but problems of health, business, home duties, or money often prevent the undertaking of a modern pilgrimage.

So I suggest you go there in imagination. By following these readings you will get an impression of what the places look like and you will need no money for fares or hotels, no passports or visas. Your home or your business will not suffer from your absence. And you will need no better health than you have now.

Your guidebook is the Bible. The logbook notes will be of little value if you do not first read the selected passages. Your guide is the Holy Spirit, so begin each reading with prayer.

Then try to live in that passage all the day, whenever you have a free moment. It is surprising how often one has to wait or go through a routine job, do household chores, or travel to and fro from work. Fill up such moments by pretending that you are in Bethlehem or Nazareth or a boat on the Sea of Galilee.

Make your own additions to the logbook, adding thoughts of your own, the verse of a hymn connected with the day's subject, a picture postcard, or an illustration from some magazine. Discuss your journey with a friend, and the Bible will come alive in a new way.

May yours be a happy pilgrimage in the Holy Land.

Beginning at Lod

The aircraft touched down at Lod Airport, a few miles from Lydda, the first town mentioned in our reading today. Lydda was originally called Lod. It was a village belonging to the tribe of Benjamin, to which the remnants of that tribe returned with joy after the captivity in Babylon. The new state of Israel gave the airport the old historic name, while the town retains its New Testament name, Lydda. A happy thought to keep both names. Lydda has many associations for the Christian world and Lod is once more a place of return from exile, new life, new service, a second chance.

Lydda is a hot, dusty town with narrow streets and flat-roofed houses. The windows mostly face into courtyards, which makes the houses look like fortresses. Those stone houses were built in the time of the Crusades and they have not changed much since. In the first century the town may have been less warlike, but it had the same flat roofs and narrow streets.

The country between Lydda and Joppa is a fertile land called the Plain of Sharon. Those verses in the Song of Solomon show that Sharon was a land of flowers and fruit centuries before the time of Christ. Today it is rich in olive trees, banana groves, orange and lemon plantations, peach and apricot orchards. The world famous Jaffa oranges come from there, called after another town in our reading. Jaffa was Joppa in the New Testament.

Jaffa, too, was rebuilt by the Crusaders and it has suffered frequently from wars throughout the centuries. Now it is merged with Tel Aviv, the largest and most modern city of Israel. So the old and the new are united, Joppa and Tel Aviv, Lydda and Lod Airport.

When Peter came down to visit the saints at Lydda, he did not find exceptional people with haloes round their heads. The saints were just everyday men, women, and children who believed in the Lord Jesus Christ and tried to serve him. Aeneas was a weak sort of saint, discouraged after eight long years of illness. He must have heard tales of the wonderful healing miracles which Jesus had performed, but at least six years earlier Jesus had been crucified. People said he had risen from the dead, but Jesus, alive or dead, never came to Lydda, and Aeneas was almost losing hope of ever being cured.

Then Peter came to Lydda and told the saints there of the wonderful outpouring of the Holy Spirit.

"Aeneas, Jesus Christ maketh thee whole; arise, and make thy bed." What Jesus had done for others when he was on earth, he still could do through the Holy Spirit. The trembling of the palsy ceased; strength flowed into the weak limbs. Life began again.

A few miles away in Joppa by the sea, Dorcas lay dead. Through Christ she was restored to life and found a new opportunity for service to others.

Christianity is not just a matter of historical interest. Christ is of vital importance in our lives today. Those events of two thousand years ago concern us now. The old and the new depend upon one another.

Jesus Christ is still able to save to the uttermost. His servants through the power of the Holy Spirit can strengthen the weak, discouraged believer. Those whose service for Christ seems at an end can find new life. The exile, defeated and in bondage to sin, can hear the call to return to the homeland of the soul.

We do not read that the Lord Jesus visited Lydda or Joppa during his earthly life but he commissioned his disciples to be his witnesses. Perhaps you are meant to be a Peter and to bring the message of new life to others.

Whatever be your need, Jesus Christ can satisfy if you give him your faith and obedience. Aeneas must have felt himself a pretty useless witness. Read verse 35 once more and see what happened at Lydda as a result of his taking the Lord at his word. All that dwelt at Lydda saw him and turned to the Lord.

New life and new opportunities of service for you!

A Roman Capital

Bird watching is a favorite hobby nowadays. The first birds we saw in the Holy Land were sparrows, multitudes of them. Palestinian sparrows prefer to fly in flocks and congregate in vast numbers, so it is no wonder the psalmist noticed a solitary sparrow sitting alone upon the housetop (Ps. 102:7). Jesus also mentioned those seemingly unimportant little brown birds, recalling even the price in the markets, two for a farthing and sometimes five for two farthings, yet not forgotten by God and that included the odd one thrown in for nothing.

We came to Caesarea in brilliant sunshine. It is a city of ruins now but during the Roman occupation it was the capital of Palestine, the official residence of the Procurators, where Pontius Pilate had his fine dwelling. Quite recently a stone with an inscription bearing his name was discovered in the ruins. The harbor used to be busy with ships from all parts of the world. Caesarea boasted a royal palace, a fine heathen temple, a hippodrome. It was the headquarters of the Roman army in Palestine. Life swarmed there, abundant, luxurious, highly civilized and utterly materialistic.

Now nothing but ruins remain.

The blue waters of the Mediterranean wash over great blocks of stone, all that is left of the ancient harbor. Seashells and sand drift over the roadway where Roman chariots once passed proudly by. Vestiges of a later city built by the Crusaders stand empty and desolate by the golden shore. The only sign of life we saw that day was a green lizard darting over a stretch of mosaic flooring, twisting his lithe body among broken marble pillars and headless porphyry statues, the remnants of the open-air theatre where the Romans held their entertainments.

Cornelius the centurion was posted to Caesarea and he lived there among all the temptations of a soldier's life. Many a young man stationed far from home drifts into sin, yet many try to live the Christian life in the army. Cornelius had no Christian background but he longed to find the true God and to live a life of righteousness. Righteousness is not a popular word in the twentieth century; it was not popular in the first. Cornelius must have had to face ridicule, which is sometimes harder to bear than persecution, but he remained faithful and continued to seek God, praying constantly and helping those in need. This faithful soldier received a greater reward than he expected. He was brought to know Christ the Savior of the world as his own Savior. He became the first Gentile to be officially received into the Christian church.

The silent, dead city lies in ruins. The centurion Cornelius will live forever.

Do you sometimes feel like an unimportant sparrow among the swarming multitudes on earth? Do you feel yourself to be an exile, placed in a position where temptation seems almost too strong? Have you ever wondered whether your prayers were any use at all?

Loneliness will pass away. The fiercest temptations will come to an end. The material importance of this life will fade into an oblivion greater than that of beautiful Caesarea.

But: "They that be wise shall shine as the brightness of the firmament; and they that turn many to righteousness as the stars for ever and ever" (Dan. 12:3).

Mount Carmel

Read today's passage aloud if you have an opportunity. It is one of the finest dramas in all literature, vivid action set upon a magnificent stage. Picture to yourself the rugged prophet of the Lord on that wild, lonely hillside facing the might of King Ahab with his four hundred and fifty idolatrous prophets of Baal and four hundred prophets of the groves, servants of the heathen Queen Jezebel.

Mount Carmel is a ridge stretching inland for about fifteen miles and forming a bold promontory on the coast. In Old Testament times it was well forested, and Elijah and the Baal prophets must have found plenty of wood for all the sacrifices there. Isaiah 35:2 speaks of the excellence of Carmel and Sharon. Micah 7:14 mentions the wood in the midst of Carmel, so it must have been a beauty spot in those days. If you stand on the top of Carmel, the highest point overlooking the Mediterranean, you can feel the scorching sunshine and the salt tang of the sea just as Elijah did.

In some ways, though, the scenery has changed. Instead of scrambling up five hundred feet of rock-strewn wilderness, you can drive through a smart residential area of Haifa, the second largest city in Israel, passing modern white houses set in gardens gay with crimson or pink oleander, petunia-colored bougainvillaea, and blue jacaranda. You can reach the summit by a mountain railway and see the elaborate church and the Institute of Technology. Or you can visit the cave traditionally associated with Elijah. It was a dark shrine and when we arrived there, a monk was dusting the black stone statue of the prophet with a feather brush!

The heights of Carmel make an impressive site for a ceremony. Various sects and religions still have their centers on the Mount. Elijah realized the strategic value of the position when he requested Ahab to summon all Israel and the prophets of Baal and of the groves to come up there to answer his ringing challenge: "How long halt ye between two opinions? if the Lord be God, follow him: but if Baal, then follow him."

Baal worship was the fashionable religion in those days. Queen Jezebel was very powerful and Ahab was weak and under her thumb. Very few people dared to oppose the wealthy and influential ruling class. There were a hundred prophets of the Lord whom Obadiah had hidden in a cave and, known only to God, there were seven thousand in all Israel who had not bowed the knee to Baal. However, up there on Mount Carmel, Elijah was standing alone.

The fanatic, the people must have thought him. It is *so* hard to be different. We find it just the same today though the worship of Baal has ceased. Other idols claim our allegiance; a desire to be popular, though innocent at first, may grow to a lust for power, to ruthless selfishness, to cruel ambition. The love of money is the root of all evil; covetousness is idolatry. Jesus warned us that hidden thoughts become sinful actions. The last words of John's first Epistle are, "Keep yourselves from idols."

So the message of Elijah is for us today. If the Lord be God, follow him. A greater sacrifice than that of Elijah's bullocks has been offered, a sacrifice which can free us from the power of sin. On the cross of Calvary Christ died to break that power.

14

Nazareth

Nazareth is quite a large town now. It nestles among the green hills so peacefully that one expects to find devout faces and the music of church bells. There were churches in abundance, but when we came to Nazareth a street fight was going on, the sort of gang warfare that happens everywhere among young folk. Stones were thrown and shouts echoed down the narrow streets and through the crowded bazaar. We wanted to putter about in the Suk, looking at the open stalls with their odd assortment of wares, oriental embroideries, transistor radios, Arab sweetmeats, ice-cream cornets, camels carved in wood or ivory, joints of meat, brassware, bicycles, bead necklaces, carpets. Our guide, however, hustled us into a church to keep us out of the way while the riot went on. We never found out what caused the quarrel or how it ended. The shouting seemed to be in a variety of languages, since people come from all over the world to visit Nazareth.

We saw the famous well from which Mary must have drawn her water, probably taking the child Jesus with her. It is still the only well in Nazareth, though piped water has been brought into the town, too. Nazareth is a town greatly honored, since it can claim among its citizens the One Man who passed through childhood, boyhood, adolescence, and

15

young manhood without stain of sin. Yet above the town stands the hill from whose brow the people of Nazareth once tried to cast down the Holy One. The home town of Jesus rejected him.

Isn't that true to life! Home is not the easiest place in which to live as a true Christian. It is more pleasant to witness among strangers than among those who know us too well. Jesus found opposition at home, and his own brothers did not understand him. In the synagogue when the Carpenter of Nazareth made his great claim to be the fulfillment of Isaiah's prophecy, he was howled down and thrown out. Life was not easy for Jesus. He was tempted in all points as we are. When he returned to Nazareth, he could do no mighty work there because of unbelief. A few sick folk were healed but most were offended at him. None of his brothers were included among the twelve chosen Apostles.

No mighty work? In his own good time the mighty work was wrought by the loving Savior of mankind.

After the crucifixion and the resurrection of our Lord, his brothers joined him along with Mary his mother and the other disciples. James became a leader in the early church. Jude became the writer of the last of the Epistles. Notice how he begins that letter: "Jude, the servant of Jesus Christ, and brother of James." Unbelief has vanished. Humbly Jude rejoices to serve Jesus as Lord and Master.

And the home town? We do not read in the Bible that the people of Nazareth were all converted then but that generation must have heard with awe and wonder the story of their one-time carpenter. Throughout the centuries, even when the country was under Moslem rule, Nazareth was known as a Christian town.

Was that in answer to the prayers of the greatest of her citizens? Did Jesus plead for his unbelieving city when he climbed the hills a great while before dawn?

On the cross at Golgotha, Jesus ended his earthly life with words from a simple prayer taught to all Jewish boys. He probably learned it in Nazareth at his mother's knee. He may have heard young James and Jude, Simon, Joses and his sisters repeating the same words at bedtime. "Father into thy hands I commend my spirit." In the darkness on that cross, he may have thought of those days of childhood, of friends long ago who had not accepted him.

I think the folk of Nazareth were included in that other prayer from the cross: "Father forgive them for they know not what they do."

So do not be discouraged if friends, family, or neighbors don't think much of your Christian life. Go on praying for them and for those who manage the affairs of your town and your country and for the leaders of your church. You cannot tell what the result of those prayers will be. But God can.

Wedding at Cana

Night comes swiftly in the East. We left Nazareth and its crowded streets and dark pointed cypress trees in the afternoon. Evening fell as we drove along a road winding among the hills. In the gathering dusk we saw pelicans and cranes feeding in a swamp. Then suddenly it was night. The sky was like black velvet, pierced with diamond stars.

"This is Cana of Galilee," said the guide when the coach stopped. "You may get out here and drink from the well whose waters were once changed into wine."

We stumbled over the grass, groping our way in the dark. Some girls came running towards us with water pots offering to draw water for the travelers, and we stood by the village well for a drink. The water was certainly not wine now, for it tasted musty and stale, but this was the place of the miracle since it is the only well in Cana. Perhaps the water was clearer in those days when it was not so often disturbed by parties of pilgrims or tourists. There must have been water in plenty then, for six water pots of stone had been filled to the brim at the command of Jesus, giving wine enough to gladden the wedding feast.

The girls had left their cottage door wide open and we could see a family laughing together as they ate their supper

19

by the light of a lamp. The family which welcomed Jesus and his disciples to the wedding must have been just such a cheery crowd, hospitable even to the point of inviting more guests than they could afford to entertain. Perhaps there were some gate crashers at the wedding breakfast or else the hosts were too poor to buy wine for all who turned up.

Mary realized what had gone wrong. With ready sympathy she understood the humiliation of her friends when supplies ran short, and she knew exactly what to do and how to help. Now this was a big step of faith. Jesus had as yet performed no miracles, but his life in Nazareth had been so full of loving service to others that his mother knew she could rely on his help.

She took the critical situation to Jesus. And that spoiled wedding became a wedding of wonderful blessing.

Wedding ceremonies cause much anxiety. Marriage seems to be rather a toss up. Poverty can mar the happiness of a home. Selfishness can break up an ideal union. Some are not given the joy of married life. Others lose that joy all too soon. The wells give only water and there is no more wine.

Mary knew what to do. She told Jesus and waited for him to act, wisely advising the servants, "Whatsoever he saith unto you, do it."

Those servants must have been puzzled when they were told to draw water from the well, but they obeyed without question. So they too had the honor of sharing the miracle with Jesus.

The ruler of the feast, master of ceremonies, did not know where the best wine came from, but the servants who drew the water knew.

Wouldn't you like to have been one of those servants?

Countless marriages at the present time are threatened with disaster. Everywhere men and women are facing disappointment, humiliation, despair. If you know of any homes where there is trouble and anxiety, tell Jesus. Then, "Whatsoever he saith unto you, do it."

The Sermon
On the Mount

For three days we stayed in a quiet hospice on the hill known as the Mount of Beatitudes. From a seat on the low wall of the garden we could see the lake which Jesus knew so well.

The path leading down to the shore winds through the olive trees and flowering shrubs of the garden, past the hospice chapel and on among green fields down toward the Sea of Galilee. In the time of Christ, many towns and villages bordered the lake: Capernaum, Bethsaida, Chorazin, and others. All but Tiberias have disappeared, though here and there new buildings have arisen. The shores of Galilee are peaceful and quiet in spite of modern developments, so one has to use his imagination to think of those lost towns when reading of the multitudes who gathered to hear the words of Jesus and to be healed of their diseases.

On a clear day you can see the snow-capped summits of Mount Hermon, the highest range in Palestine afar in the north. On the eastern shore low red-brown hills shine eight miles away, while the hills of Galilee in the west cast long

21

shadows over the water. Three great cranes wheel slowly across the sky, their black wings outspread, their white bodies touched with pink from the setting sun. By the water's edge, beyond a dark clump of trees, lie the ruins of Capernaum, fragments of its old synagogue, paving stones from the place where at even when the sun did set, they brought unto him all that were diseased. Along the shore southwards a small chapel marks the place where our Lord appeared to his disciples early one morning after he had risen from the dead.

It is a perfect evening in May, completely peaceful. Surely it is the summit of happiness for a Christian to be able to sit in this beautiful garden and look down upon these hallowed scenes! Happy are they who are fortunate enough to see the places where Jesus did his marvelous works; happy are the young and the strong who are able to travel and the wealthy who can afford to fly round the world; happy are the lovers of beautiful scenery. . . .

No! I have it all wrong. That is not what Jesus said.

When Jesus sat on this same hillside and looked down on the shimmering lake, away to snowy Hermon, to the rust-red hills and the busy villages, he told his followers what was the secret of true happiness.

Happy are the poor in spirit: for theirs is the kingdom of heaven.

Happy are they that mourn: for they shall be comforted.

Happy are the meek: for they shall inherit the earth.

Happy are they which do hunger and thirst after righteousness: for they shall be filled.

Happy are the merciful: for they shall obtain mercy.

Happy are the pure in heart: for they shall see God.

Happy are the peacemakers: for they shall be called the children of God.

Happy are they which are persecuted for righteousness' sake: for their's is the kingdom of heaven.

Happy are ye, when men shall revile you, and persecute you, and shall say all manner of evil against you falsely, for my sake (Matt. 5:3-11).

Happy? How can anyone be happy when he is persecuted and slandered? One who mourns cannot be happy.

The word Jesus used is not what we mean by happy. Happiness passes. Age, poverty, distress, bereavement, cruelty from others, betrayal by friends: all these can destroy happiness. Blessedness is permanent, a joy which will endure through all sorrow and which lasts for evermore.

In His presence is fullness of joy.

Rejoice, and be exceeding glad: for great is your reward in heaven.

And when you have time to spare, read through the Book of the Acts of the Apostles and notice every time *rejoice* and *rejoicing* and *joy* are mentioned. The apostles heard that sermon on the Mount, and they lived it out in their lives.

Day 7—Mark 1:21-34

Capernaum

When Nazareth rejected our Lord, he made Capernaum the center of his early ministry. Capernaum had a good position on the shores of the lake and was a busy place with a new synagogue built by a Roman centurion friendly to the Jews. The people welcomed Jesus at first and crowded in such numbers to see and hear him that he had to continue his work outside the town.

The path down to the ruins of the town led through a banana grove and plantations of orange and lemon trees. It wound over sun-baked fields where grew tangles of wild oats, blue thistles like huge balls, and masses of other summer flowers. May in Palestine is a hot, dry month, the time of the barley harvest. The fields of barley were indeed "white unto harvest," but the day we passed that way we saw no reapers.

By the water a couple of shepherd boys were tending flocks of black goats and thin sheep with long, silky yellow ears. A monk came out of the chapel to show us the ruins of the synagogue, and a few tourists stood nearby taking photographs of the few remaining pillars and the threshold of the one entrance, pointed out as the only stone upon which it is certain that Jesus once stood. The rest of Capernaum had vanished as Jesus foretold:

"And thou, Capernaum, which art exalted unto heaven, shalt be brought down to hell: for if the mighty works, which have been done in thee, had been done in Sodom, it would have remained until this day" (Matt. 11:23).

In that synagogue Jesus himself had preached. In the houses whose walls have crumbled to dust the centurion's servant had been healed, a dead child had been restored to life, Peter's mother-in-law and the man let down through the roof had been given health and strength again. In the vanished streets many sick folk had risen up cured at eventide.

Did those miracles make Capernaum blaze forth the wonder that the Son of God was there? Did the townsfolk send the story ringing round the world and leave their homes to spread the good news?

Matthew the tax gatherer was one who did. He did not hesitate to quit his job, though he was probably making big money at it. How grateful we are for the Gospel he wrote, using the education he had acquired to make a careful detailed account of the coming of the Messiah to the Jews and the Savior to the world! He remembered certain words of our Lord and incidents which were not recorded in the other Gospels. It is quite possible that he knew Joseph and heard from him the story of the wondrous birth and the coming of the wise men. I am so glad that he recorded those words of comfort in Matthew 11:28-30. How many thousands of weary and anxious people have been helped by them.

We do not know the names of the four friends who brought the palsied man to Jesus, but their ingenuity in letting him down through the roof has made their memory live forever in the minds of Christians. Jairus and his wife and their little daughter, the centurion and his servant, Peter's grateful family, all these we know as dear friends, but what about the others who found health in those cool evenings? What about the civic authorities who must have known who was doing these miracles?

The majority of the inhabitants of Capernaum saw the miracles, stared and gossiped, and went on with their ordinary affairs. What could they do: busy housewives, fishermen, tradesmen, farmers?

What difference does one reaper make in a harvest field? In these days, of course, he can reap it all alone with his combine harvester, but there were no tractors or machines then. A crowd of reapers went out with their sickles, each to do his appointed section of the harvest.

To your care God has entrusted one corner of the harvest field of the world. You are called to serve Christ by sowing the seed, spreading the good news, or by reaping your part of the harvest of souls, just where you are. You may feel you have only a sickle instead of a combine harvester, that your work is of little importance, but it is your work. Nobody else can do it.

Somewhere upon a bare hillside,
  Above the lake that gleamed below,
A peasant sowed at morning-tide
  His field, and Jesus watched him sow.

Far are the hills of Galilee,
  That harvest long is reaped, but still
Jesus is watching us, as we
  Sow in his field for good or ill.
                    —Author Unknown

On the Shore

There are many seashore stories in the Gospels: the calling of Simon and Andrew as they waded in the shallows, casting their nets for a catch; the story of James and John in the boat with their father mending their nets, for nets easily get torn and are costly to buy. And there are the stories of the boat borrowed to be used as a pulpit by Jesus, and the great multitude of fishes caught after a night of fishing in vain. Perhaps the most beautiful is the story of the picnic breakfast on the seashore, the glad surprise of that morning when the risen Lord appeared once more to his friends.

They are all morning stories. At night the storms at sea and the walking on the water, but in the morning came the challenge to youth, "Follow me and I will make you fishers of men."

Not far from Capernaum there is a little bay framed in golden blossoms hanging from the trees which arch the pebbly strand. To reach it you must pass through a wood where seven springs gurgle from the rocks among clusters of maidenhair fern and tall spires of wild blue delphiniums. When Irene and I walked down there, we saw fishing nets hanging out to dry on the stone breakwater and the clear water rippled gently against the side of a boat drawn up beside it. An old man was sitting on a boulder, deep in meditation. He had come to the Holy Land as a fulfillment of a lifelong desire. A minister, eighty years of age, he had been a fisher of men for most of his life.

It was Friday, the Jewish Sabbath, and this bay is believed to be the place where Jesus hailed his tired, disappointed disciples and welcomed them to the breakfast he had prepared. A small chapel has been built to commemorate the event. In the middle of its floor there is a great slab of unhewn rock, said to be the spot where Jesus made a fire of coals and prepared a meal of bread and fish. When we went in, four young clergymen from the United States were kneeling around that rock while one of them read aloud the story of that morning of glad surprise.

"When the morning was now come, Jesus stood on the shore" (John 21:4).

"He leadeth me beside the still waters. He restoreth my soul" (Ps. 23:2).

Three times Peter had denied his Lord and now he was given three opportunities of declaring his love once more, and three times he was encouraged by being given work to do in his dear Master's service.

We all need restoration of soul. Impulsive, eager-hearted Peter had failed and then had repented with bitter tears. Even John the beloved disciple had forsaken the Lord in the Garden of Gethsemane. Thomas had doubted. Nathanael who had once been highly praised by Jesus was not brave enough to face danger for Christ's sake. We have all failed our Master in some way, the young and the old.

The fishers of men who started out so gallantly with such high ideals, such glowing faith, have had a long dark night and have returned with empty nets. Was it all for nothing, those hopes and prayers, the joyous witness and the radiant fellowship?

"But when the morning was now come, Jesus stood on the shore." And to us, as to the fishermen of old, he says: "Lovest thou me? . . . Follow me . . . Feed my sheep."

30

The Country

Of the Gadarenes

There is only one place on the far side of the lake where there is a cliff steep enough for the swine in this story to have met their end. I used to be puzzled by the fate of these poor creatures until I found out more about the background of the incident. The swine was an unclean animal according to the law of Moses, and the Jews were forbidden to eat the flesh or even to touch the carcass of the pig. Moses was a great leader, trained in all the wisdom of the highly civilized Egyptian court, as well as being inspired by the Holy Spirit of God. In that hot country when refrigeration was not known, it would have been highly dangerous to sit down to a meal of pork or bacon or brawn! Even within living memory, it was the custom in northern lands never to eat pork when there was no "R" in the month, that is during the summer season. Our Lord knew that the owners of those swine kept them for sale, making profit out of the danger to men's lives and he gave the poor creatures the quickest and most painless death. His action was not cruelty, but kindness.

We crossed the lake in a motorboat from Capernaum to the modern village of Ein Gev, not far from the cliff known as the Steeps of Gadara. Ein Gev is a prosperous place with a fine Kibbutz, one of the many Israeli settlements for agricultural workers, very well equipped. An American millionaire built a theatre at Ein Gev in which a musical festival is held in the spring and entertainments are given for the workers in the Kibbutz. There are gardens and amusement parks. The Jews of today live a very different life from that of the lonely demoniac who made his home among the tombs in the desolate hills. Yet the modern Israeli has his problems, too, and in spite of culture and education, he must be ever watchful, ever alert, ever ready to defend his home.

Many Jews today ask the same question as that poor tormented man, "What have I to do with thee, Jesus?"

All the more liberal Jews accept Jesus as one of the great heroes of their nation, though few add with the uncanny insight of the wild demoniac, "What have I to do with thee, Jesus, thou Son of the most high God."

Devil possession is hard to understand in the quiet of civilized life, but when war and revolution break out, it is seen most clearly.

The peaceful lake over which we had passed changed suddenly on the return journey. The wind rose and waves splashed over the sides. To add to the trouble the engine broke down. It was only a summer storm, not a violent tempest, but as we tossed on the Sea of Galilee we thought of Jesus stilling the winds and the waves once long ago and of the soul tempest he had stilled up there on the Steeps of Gadara. That distressed man may once have been an innocent child in a happy country home. Now his innocence had gone. He had given way to sin and devils had taken possession. This was no case of simple mental illness. Tormented in mind and in soul, he came out from his dwelling among the rock tombs and met with Jesus.

No case is too hard for the Lord. Fetters and chains could not hold this man, but Jesus could reach to the hidden depths of his misery. Jesus, the same yesterday, today, and forever, is still ready to calm the troubled mind, to pardon the sinner, to speak peace to the sufferer, to evict the devils from souls possessed, and to bring out the very best from those who feel themselves inferior. No complex is too hard for the Lord.

Material comfort cannot still the storms of life. The wealthiest people are often the most unhappy. Only the peace of God which passeth understanding can still the tempests of sorrow, sin, and shame. Only the peace which Jesus gives can strengthen us in time of suffering and in the hour of death.

The River Jordan

We saw the Jordan twice, first where it flows gently out of the Sea of Galilee, and later at its mouth, where it enters the Dead Sea. The Jordan is a strange river, rising on the eastern side of Mount Hermon, the snow-capped giant far in the north. Coming from those snows, the river winds into a swampy plain, forming a lake known as the Waters of Merom or Lake Huleh. From Huleh it increases in volume and force and flows on into the Sea of Galilee and out again at the southern end. Then in a series of corkscrew windings the river descends rapidly, falling 600 feet in 60 miles and comes to an end in the Dead Sea, from which there is no outlet, except by evaporation.

The river is not really wide, nor exceptionally long. Between the two seas, its course is through thick jungle, known as "The Pride of Jordan." Here flowering trees and bushes grow in profusion and the heat is intense, though the river always looks cool beneath the green shadows. Once lions and other wild animals lurked there, but now the river is being made use of by scientific means. Jordan, the Descender as its name means, is small and insignificant but it is probably the best known river in the world.

Naaman the Syrian did not think much of the turgid, muddy waters of Jordan. He was too proud to dip himself in such a stream, even if by so doing he could be cured of his leprosy.

"Are not Abana and Pharpar, rivers of Damascus, better than all the waters of Israel? may I not wash in them and be clean?"

But the haughty Syrian captain found that there was no cleansing for him unless he humbled himself and dipped seven times in Jordan. The story of Naaman is a picture of another river whose waters can heal a disease worse than leprosy. As William Cowper's old hymn says:

There is a fountain filled with blood
Drawn from Immanuel's veins;
And sinners, plunged beneath that flood,
Lose all their guilty stains.

There is no other way to be cleansed from sin but by the precious blood shed on Calvary. Good works, bitter remorse, earnest prayers, and striving after holiness cannot take away sin. The sinless Son of God needed no repentance and had no sins to confess, yet, as our representative, he submitted himself to baptism in the Jordan and took the sinner's place in its waters. That baptism is for us a symbol of the finished work of atonement when he took the sinner's place upon the cross and bore the punishment for our sins.

The wonder of it! That He who created all things, one with the Father and the Holy Spirit, should submit to this for me!

Thou dying Lamb, thy precious blood
Shall never lose its power,
Till all the ransomed church of God
Are saved, to sin no more.

E'er since by faith I saw the stream
Thy flowing wounds supply,
Redeeming love has been my theme
And shall be till I die.

36

Zion

Psalms 120 to 134 are called the Songs of Degrees, or Ascents because they were sung by pilgrims climbing to Jerusalem. "Whither the tribes go up" describes the journey, for you have to climb, whichever way you enter the city. Jesus must have repeated Psalm 122 when, as a boy, he first approached Jerusalem, and again whenever he returned there.

Mount Zion is the highest point of the city and for many years it remained unconquered, the stronghold of the Jebusites, an impregnable fortress. King David took it by storm. When the Romans destroyed Jerusalem in A.D. 70, they piled up the ruins to level and hide forever the remains of such a rebellious place. They failed to level Mount Zion. Buildings they could knock down, but not the stronghold.

There are fine buildings in the Jerusalem of the Israelis: modern houses, shops, the Knesset, the Government house, museums, and the great Hebrew University on Mount Scopus, but as we climbed up to Zion we passed a housing estate erected before the Great War for Jews who wished to live in their homeland. The millionaire Montefiore realized the dangers and difficulties for Jews living there and made good preparations.

Our guide pointed out a large square stone in the roadway covered by a padlocked iron lid.

"See that? It is a cistern. In 1948, there was fighting here in this quarter. It was besieged. Water was cut off. People here must die. But they did not die! Why? I tell you why. Under this big stone there is cistern. Water there, hidden water. Water that saved the people."

One greater than kind-hearted Montefiore has provided for all the world the Fountain of Living Water. Jesus said: "Whosoever drinketh of the water that I shall give him shall never thirst; but the water that I shall give him shall be in him a well of water springing up into everlasting life" (John 4:14).

We climbed on up in the blazing heat. Presently we came to wide easy steps which the Israeli government had put up to help weary pilgrims on the steepest part of the ascent. The guide pointed to the huge, solid foundation stones used in the building of a Crusader church.

"Strong foundations," he said. "But I say no more. Sometimes I tell you things. Sometimes I say nothing. The stones speak."

The stones of Jerusalem speak, as Jesus said they would, crying out in witness to the truth, speaking of the Savior who lived his earthly life in that land and who loved that great city. They speak also of his church on earth, the mystical body of all believers, built upon the foundation of the Apostles and prophets, Jesus Christ himself being the Chief Corner Stone.

"They that trust in the Lord shall be as mount Zion, which cannot be removed, but abideth for ever (Ps. 125:1).

Two Upper Rooms

On Mount Zion there are two famous Upper Rooms, besides other sacred sites. There is an amazing contrast between the two.

The Chamber of Destruction is a memorial to the sufferings of the six million Jews who perished during the Nazi persecutions. Pathetic relics of the agony of concentration camps and extermination centers are displayed in a dark rock chamber, lit by guttering olive oil candles. Tablets of soap made by the persecutors from dead bodies, blood-stained clothing, half-burnt precious scrolls of the Law, and other terrible mementos of those cruel times are preserved to remind the world of the bitter suffering which Jews have so bravely faced throughout the ages. Persecuted but not destroyed! The race survives. They are God's Chosen People, even though they have rejected the Messiah.

Nearby stands the other Upper Room, known as the Coenaculum, the room said to be that in which our Lord ate the Last Supper with his disciples. It cannot be at all like the original room, for Crusaders built a church over the site, and the Mohammedans turned the church into a mosque. Now it is neither church nor mosque. It stands empty and services are not permitted there to avoid strife. Though this room has no resemblance to the guestchamber lent to the Lord for that Passover meal, yet it is still a sacred place, reminding Christians of what happened here or near this spot.

Standing on the bare paving stones in this big empty room, we considered a very different memorial. In the room of the Last Supper, Jesus knowing that he was about to die, girded himself with a towel and knelt in love to wash the feet of his disciples. Here, facing the bitterest treachery, he gave the sop to Judas, a last gentle warning to the traitor that there was still time to repent. Here Jesus spoke wonderful words of comfort to the friends he was soon to leave. Here he inaugurated the service of Holy Communion which has united believers with one another and with their crucified and risen Savior from that day on. Here, it is believed, was the place where the Holy Spirit descended upon the waiting disciples at Pentecost.

One room is a memorial of the utmost cruelty, torture, and agony; the other is a memorial of love and forgiveness beyond all telling.

And Jesus passed through both. In the darkness of the cross when he cried out, "My God, my God, why hast thou forsaken me?" he was bearing the sin of the whole world, suffering not only physical agony but also the deepest spiritual distress. He knows suffering. He understands.

Mount of Scandal

"You must learn to speak Hebrew if you are going to spend some time in Israel!" Well-meant advice, but not easy to carry out. Hebrew is a difficult language. Yet we all know quite a number of Hebrew words which have entered into the English tongue. Manna, Messiah, Rabbi, Selah, Seraph, Sabbath, Amen, Hallelujah, Hosanna, Jubilee—all these came from the Hebrew. Here is another word frequently heard in Israel, *Shalom*. Shalom is the word of greeting in the Holy Land and it means "Peace."

We stayed on the outskirts of Jerusalem in a hotel on the Mount of Scandal, not a very pleasant name for a mountain, though the situation was excellent with a good view of the Mount of Olives and of the walled city. With a name like that, one would hardly expect to find peace. A party of pilgrims rent by gossip and spiteful words, were we? Or were we torn by distinctions of color, class, or denomination? No, we were a happy group, and that hotel among the olive trees on the hill outside the wall was for us a holy place.

Was it due to the fact that every morning was hallowed very early by our meeting at the Lord's table. The simple service of Holy Communion united us with our Savior as we remembered what he had done for us on that other hill of

41

Calvary not far away. Our morning services were held in a chapel dedicated to Saint Ephraim, a Syrian hymn-writer of the fourth century. The hotel had once been a monastery belonging to the Greek Church and the chapel in the basement remained, decorated with strange, bright-colored wall-paintings, an unusual place of worship for most of us. As we traveled, we had to adapt ourselves to strange places of worship. In Galilee we met in the open air, on the hills above the lake, kneeling on the stony ground beneath aged olive trees. The place might vary, but that gathering together with our Lord to begin the day bound us in fellowship with one another.

The Mount of Scandal, though, did remind us that there are many people whose lives are wrecked by the distress caused by the unkind words of others. Scandal is hard to endure and only the Holy Spirit can give us strength to suffer without bitterness.

The psalmist gives very practical advice about this very trouble, so relevant in these modern days.

"Fret not thyself."

"Trust in the Lord."

"Delight thyself in the Lord."

"Commit thy way unto the Lord."

"Rest in the Lord."

"Wait patiently for him."

"Cease from anger."

In short, keep looking to Jesus, and don't dwell on the unkindness of others. The two verses in Psalm 31 show what God will do for those who trust in him. He has a hiding place for troubled souls. In the secret of his presence there is rest. The pavilion was the tabernacle, the tent church which traveled with the Israelites during their long wanderings in the wilderness. Whatever our troubles may be and wherever we are, the Christian always has a secret refuge, a place of meeting with God.

The Old City

There are many modern buildings in Jerusalem now, but much of the ancient city remains. When you enter by the famous Damascus Gate, you leave the twentieth century with its traffic problems behind and step right into the East as it used to be. Cars, trucks, or motor vans cannot use these narrow streets, and heavily laden donkeys come charging along, their riders screaming and booing at the pedestrians, urging them to get out of the way, and at the double, too. Not that there is much room to step aside, for rows of old men sit on low stools before the open shops, smoking hookahs and gossiping. Children swarm everywhere; veiled women are still seen, swinging by with graceful movements. A water carrier can sometimes even now be heard, yelling his age-old call: "Ho, every one that thirsteth, come ye to the waters!" (Isa. 55:1).

Jerusalem is a strange medley of East and West nowadays. Tourists with their cameras mingle with sheikhs, bird sellers, pastry cooks carrying trays of sweetmeats on their heads, Bedouins from the country visiting the town, soldiers, priests of many differing faiths, nuns, monks, beggars, television teams, visitors from all over the world. Gramophones and radios blare from shops and houses and portable transistors. Everyone has to shout to get a hearing!

Sunblinds overhead make streaks of shadow alternating with brilliant sunshine. The noisy Suk, or bazaar is full of life, and from it one turns into the stillness of the Via Dolorosa, a narrow street built as far as one can tell in the direction of the ancient road along which Jesus passed on the way to Calvary. The actual road would be deep beneath the present street level.

How the Jewish race has always loved this ancient city! Always it must have been a place of strife, warfare—a turbulent city, with its swarming multitudes and milling crowds. Being a place of pilgrimage, it was a center for travelers from every part of the known world in our Lord's lifetime. Jews would come up for the great feasts to worship in the glorious temple which crowned Mount Moriah. Jesus loved Jerusalem. He wept over the careless indifference of its inhabitants and the hard self-righteousness of those who felt they had no need of him and his great love.

"O Jerusalem, Jerusalem, thou that killest the prophets, and stonest them which are sent unto thee, how often would I have gathered thy children together, even as a hen gathereth her chickens under her wings, and ye would not" (Matt. 24:37).

Will you pray for the peace of Jerusalem tonight, for the peace of the city which Jesus loved long ago and still loves today!

We have read how Nicodemus came to Jesus by night, stealthily, that his visit might not be noticed, or possibly choosing a time when he could see the Master alone. Was he afraid of criticism as he walked through the deserted streets? Or was Nicodemus longing to find peace in that restless city named for peace? He came by night, but he came. That is what mattered. And his talk with Jesus that night has brought countless thousands to find eternal life.

All the Jews did not reject Jesus. Your prayers may bring some twentieth century Nicodemus to him tonight.

The Golden Gate

It was Irene's birthday and, as evening fell, we paused to gaze over the deep gorge of the Kedron valley to the city set upon a hill bathed in the glow of sunset. The eastern walls of Jerusalem have a honey-colored tint which catches the evening light, turning them to gold. I do not know whether the original Golden Gate received its name because of this coloration of the stone or whether Solomon overlaid the gate with pure gold as he did the doors of the temple building. It matters little. The gate leading from the temple area through the city wall facing the Mount of Olives has always been known as the Golden Gate and for centuries it has been closed.

Tradition says that this was the gate by which Jesus entered Jerusalem on Palm Sunday, and this tradition is probably right because that would be the obvious way from Bethany and Bethphage. There is an interesting prophecy in the Book of Ezekiel about this gate. Ezekiel in exile thought much about the beautiful temple of Solomon which had been destroyed, and he was given visions of a new and greater temple which would one day stand in the Holy Place. His visions are not easy to follow, but the gates of the temple are mentioned many times, with special reference to the gate which looked towards the east.

"And the glory of the Lord came into the house by the way of the gate whose prospect is toward the east" (Ezek. 43:4).

"Then he brought me back the way of the gate of the outward sanctuary which looketh towards the east; and it was shut.

"Then said the Lord unto me; This gate shall be shut, it shall not be opened, and no man shall enter in by it; because the Lord, the God of Israel, hath entered in by it, therefore it shall be shut.

"It is for the prince; the prince, he shall sit in it to eat bread before the Lord; he shall enter by the way of the porch of that gate" (44:1-3).

As prophesied, the gate looking toward the east has been walled up for centuries. Under Moslem rule it was feared that people might use that entry as a short cut through Al-Haram Al Sharif. The paved area where the Jewish temple once stood is a Moslem sanctuary. The beautiful Dome of the Rock covers the summit of Mount Moriah. This is where Abraham offered up Isaac, David prayed for his plague-stricken people, the Shekinah glory once shone forth.

The last remaining vestiges of the old temple foundations are known as the Wailing Wall and devout Jews come every Sabbath to weep over the destruction of their "holy and beautiful house." While the city was divided, the Wailing Wall was in Jordanian territory, but now once more the Jews are free to continue the old tradition and make their prayers and lamentations there.

The temple is destroyed: Solomon's temple, the rebuilt temple after the return from exile, and the temple built by Herod which was standing in the days of our Lord. The glory has departed. The Golden Gate is still closed, but the Christian does not need to weep and lament. Our reading today tells us of that New Jerusalem wherein is no temple, for the Lord God Almighty and the Lamb are the temple of it. There is no need of the sun to gild the walls of that city, for the Glory of God lightens it and the Lamb is the light of it.

"And the gates of it shall not be shut at all by day: for there shall be no night there."

The sunset faded and the Golden Gate grew dim. We stood in the quiet garden above the dark valley and sang of that nightless city.

> *Jerusalem the golden,*
>   *With milk and honey blest,*
> *Beneath thy contemplation*
>   *Sink heart and voice oppressed;*
> *I know not, O I know not*
>   *What joys await us there,*
> *What radiancy of glory,*
>   *What bliss beyond compare.*
>   —Bernard of Cluny

Day 16—John 18:1-2; Mark 14:32-46

Gethsemane

Gardens and vineyards are often mentioned in the Scriptures, from the garden planted eastward in Eden where mankind chose the way of sin to the garden of the empty tomb where the risen Christ conquered sin and its power. The Garden of Gethsemane is one of the most loved gardens in the world's history.

Three of the Gospels mention that Jesus and some of his disciples went to the Mount of Olives. Matthew and Mark mention the name Gethsemane and John tells us that the place was a garden. There are various gardens on the Mount of Olives, but one has always been considered the most likely to have been chosen by Jesus when he wished to withdraw from the crowds for prayer and for rest. This garden is now under the supervision of Franciscan monks and they work hard to keep it in good order.

The day of our visit, unfortunately, the key of the gate was not available, so, much disappointed, we had to be satisfied with peering through the iron railings to see what we could. The monks, tending the flowers inside seemed unconcerned about pilgrims being locked out. I expect they were too busy for visitors. Gardening can be a backaching chore and there was much to do.

The actual garden is small, for a church has been built on the site, taking up the greater part of the hillside there. In the center of the lawn a group of twisted and gnarled old olive trees is all that can have any connection with the original garden. They are said to be old enough to have been full-grown trees at the time when Jesus often resorted there with his disciples. If this is so, those same trees must have witnessed the agony of the Savior on the eve of the crucifixion. The flower borders were not at all as one would imagine them, but they were very gay with a profusion of geraniums, scarlet lilies, flaunting bushes of purple bougainvillaes and rows of gentle-eyed pansies. The roses in full bloom had exceptionally large thorns.

The Church of All Nations, built beside the Garden, is a handsome edifice. Inside it is decorated with mosaics, the blue roof being studded with glittering stars. The most impressive part of the church is a great boulder in the floor, upon which tradition says Jesus knelt to pray. Round it are iron railings made in the shape of a crown of thorns with little birds perched on the sharp prickles. Underneath the church is a cave where Jesus and his friends may have sheltered.

In these descriptions you must have noticed often the words, "perhaps," "possibly," "may have," "tradition says." Two thousand years have passed since Jesus lived in human flesh upon this earth and countless numbers of travelers have journeyed far to see the land where his earthly life was passed. To me, sunlight and shadow; the shapes of mountains, valleys, lakes and rivers; the natural colors; and the atmosphere all mean much more than buildings erected on what may have been the site of events in the life of Christ. But there are many who want to feel the certainty that this was actually the spot where such an event happened. Guesswork has caused much confusion, but the site of the Garden of Gethsemane is not in doubt. There must have been some sort of garden there for many centuries, a garden on the slopes of the Mount of Olives separated from Jerusalem by the brook Cedron.

No one can ever fully understand the agony in the Garden. Nobody witnessed the whole of that hour of suffering, for the chosen three who were present with Jesus in that supreme moment were overcome by human weakness and fell asleep, grasping only a few of the words spoken. But how precious are the words they did catch! How many suffering souls have used Christ's prayer of Mark 14:36 when the limit of endurance has been almost reached! "Abba Father," dear Father. He knows best. In God's will is our peace. When our service for Christ grows slack and our zeal fades, how often that gentle reminder has come, "Watch and pray, lest ye enter into temptation." When our testing time seems too hard, we hear the voice of Jesus, "The spirit truly is ready, but the flesh is weak." He understands.

In that modern church, beside that neatly kept garden, it is impossible to enter fully into the agony which brought sweat like great drops of blood to Jesus' brow. We cannot take it in, but we can thank him that he bore it for our sakes.

Man became the heir to sin in a garden, bringing shame and death to the human race. Jesus in that hour of agony brought life and pardon, drinking to the dregs the cup of pain that we might know everlasting joy.

The Pavement

Did you ever play hopscotch on the sidewalks when you were a child? Did you scrawl the markings of noughts and crosses on walls or roadways? I guess not. Those old games which past generations played in city streets have no place in a civilization controlled by the use of motor transport. Children find their amusements in less dangerous playgrounds, urban streets being too busy with traffic. Yet games like that are as old as time. Archaeologists have discovered scribbled markings which prove that they were played by cavemen.

In Jerusalem in recent years evidence was found of such a game scratched in stone with some rough tool and possibly played by soldiers idly amusing themselves on the occasion of the greatest trial in history.

The convent school for girls in the famous Via Dolorosa needed modernization of its drainage system. The men working on this project had to dig through many feet of rubble underneath the school which had been built on the leveled remains of older houses erected on the ruins of the city destroyed by the Romans in A.D. 70. Hacking through piles of debris, the workmen came upon huge flagstones which appeared to be part of a vast courtyard, so they reported their find. The Mother Superior of the convent was a keen archaeologist and immediately obtained official assistance in investigating this relic of the Jerusalem of the time of our Lord. In this way was discovered the open space where Pilate sat upon his judgment seat, Gabbatha, the Pavement.

Gabbatha was an immense courtyard belonging to the fortress Antonia, where the Roman troops were garrisoned. Some of the great flagstones still show the marks of grooves made to prevent horses from slipping. Holes remain which once supported posts for barriers or standards for lamps. Gutters are still waiting to carry the scarce and valued rainwater down to great cisterns below. A few steps of the staircase are left, at the foot of which, roughly chipped into the paving stones, are the marks of a game often played by soldiers in Roman times and mentioned in classical literature, Basilicus, the Game of the King.

Standing in this underground courtyard, one can picture those soldiers. They would sit on the steps, waiting their call to duty. Idly they might watch the trial of a man known as Jesus of Nazareth, a man said to be the king of the Jews.

"King of the Jews indeed! A conquered race and a conquered king! Come, let us play Basilicus, the game of the king, and with a real king instead of an ordinary condemned criminal! Who'll take the first throw?"

With a knife or an axe, they scrawled on the stones a capital B, the sign of the game, the Star of David because their prisoner was a Jew, an eagle because he was in the power of mighty Rome, a sword for a sign of death, and a rough twisted crown of thorns for his coronation. The markings are faint after two thousand years of burial, but they can be distinguished and enough is known from Roman literature to understand how the game was played.

A prisoner condemned to death was no object of pity in those cruel days. It was fun to choose a burlesque king, to load him with mocking honors, to offer him the choice of evil pleasures, knowing that death would soon put an end to the farce. This was the game they played with Jesus and the scratchings on the stones remain.

In their coarse ignorance and cruelty the soldiers tortured the Lord of Life. Were they then the worst of men, beyond all hope of pardon? Jesus did not take that point of view. He is able to save to the uttermost. As he died, he prayed for them: "Father, forgive them, for they know not what they do."

His prayer was answered. One of the group of soldiers who watched him die was the first to acknowledge after the crucifixion that "Truly this was the Son of God."

Day 18—John 19:16-30

The Place
Of a Skull

In the fourth century when Queen Helena demanded that the Christian sites should be identified, she set the church of that time a great problem. The Romans had utterly destroyed Jerusalem and the city had been deserted for many years. After some time rebuilding began, but without any thought of reconstruction on the same plan. Houses and streets were put up over the ruins which had been simply flattened down. Of course, outstanding features could be recognized: the Mount of Olives, the Kedron Valley, Mount Zion, the Temple Courts, the Pool of Siloam, Bethesda, though the last two were not clearly visible. But how could Christians at that time be sure they knew exactly where the house with the Upper Room had stood, or where was the site of Calvary and the garden of the Resurrection, or the position of the old walls and gates?

They did their best, the monks and priests of the fourth century. It was not wise to admit ignorance to a queen, in their view, so they chose sites to show their royal visitor. The Crusaders, centuries later, found the same problem.

57

Traveling over Palestine, they felt obliged to discover long-forgotten sites of the happenings in the Old and New Testaments. Some of their choices were completely inaccurate.

The Church of the Holy Sepulchre is the traditional site of Calvary, and throughout the ages it has been a place of pilgrimage and a center of devotion. Millions have worshiped here in simple faith, but there is no evidence before that of the fourth century that this was indeed Golgotha, or Calvary, the Place of a Skull. Perhaps it does not matter much, for we know that Christ was crucified and that he rose from the dead. The actual spot where these tremendous events took place is not so important.

But to the modern pilgrim, the traditional Church of the Holy Sepulchre is a strange building. Worship there is divided among rival sects and churches. There is another site which may or may not be the true one, but which is much more as we should imagine Calvary to be.

During the time when the city was divided, a great clearance was made in order to put up a bus station. The rubble of debris removed revealed the outline of a hill always known to the Arabs as Skull Hill. It is outside the present city wall, not far from the Damascus Gate. From the Jericho Road there was a good view of the rounded shape of a low hill whose weathered rock formation gave it the appearance of a human skull with cave hollows for eyes and mouth. There had been an Arab cemetery on top, so no building was ever erected there. In the spring the grass was green with a few scanty trees. It was described by the hymn-writer, Cecil Alexander: "There is a green hill far away, outside a city wall." Skull Hill has the reputation among Arabs as having once been the site of executions, so is considered unlucky.

"And he bearing his cross went forth into a place called the place of a skull, which is called in the Hebrew Golgotha: where they crucified him."

Nearby is the cave said to be that in which Jeremiah wrote the Book of Lamentations, the saddest book in the world. Foreseeing the destruction of his beloved city, Jerusalem,

Jeremiah unwittingly foretold the far greater agony, the crucifixion of the Son of God, who looked down from that hillside to see not only Jerusalem, but the whole world threatened by destruction.

"Is it nothing to you, all ye that pass by? behold, and see if there be any sorrow like unto my sorrow" (Lam. 1:12).

That was the cry of Jeremiah, and all he could do was to bow in resignation to his misery. But Jesus passed through those hours upon the cross, bearing the sorrow and the sin of the world, and completed his work on earth with a cry of triumph, "It is finished." He had conquered sin and sorrow and death.

> *There was no other good enough*
> *To pay the price of sin;*
> *He only could unlock the gate*
> *Of heaven, and let us in.*
> —Cecil F. Alexander

And He did it for you.

The Tomb

"Now in the place where he was crucified there was a garden; and in the garden a new sepulchre, wherein was never man yet laid."

In Matthew's Gospel we find that this new sepulchre belonged to Joseph of Arimathaea and that he gave the tomb prepared for himself and his own family to be used for the burial of Jesus.

Near Skull Hill are a number of rock tombs, one of which is of particular interest. It is hewn out of the rock face in a low, sheltered site which once must have been a garden or vineyard, since there was an ancient winepress buried there. If Skull Hill is the true site of Calvary, it is very likely that this rock-hewn tomb is the one from which our Lord rose triumphant over death. Evidence points in its favor, and the proximity to Calvary combined with the peaceful seclusion of the garden now carefully maintained, make this a very hallowed spot.

This tomb must originally have been built for a man of means who could afford to be buried privately. Joseph of Arimathaea could afford a costly tomb. He was a counselor and a person of great importance among the Jews, since he could request a secret interview with Pontius Pilate, the Roman Governor. The tomb is carved out of solid rock and divided into three sections where bodies should lie, but only one was completed. This resting place must have been found too short for the body of a tall man, so a cavity to fit the head had been hastily hollowed out, without the care and neatness of the rest of the construction, as if those who were about to bury a tall man had need to hurry. The body of Jesus had to be buried in haste on account of the Jewish Sabbath which began at sunset on Friday.

Chemical tests on the stone of this grave show no trace of the decay of death. The body of Jesus was not suffered to see corruption. Rock tombs are very dark, yet the disciple who outran Peter stooped down, looked in, and saw the linen clothes lying. In the brilliant sunshine of a spring morning, it would be difficult to see into the darkness, but this tomb has a hole in the rock face which would have allowed a beam of light to pierce the gloom.

There are no records to prove that the Garden Tomb is the actual one in which the body of our Lord was laid, but with such evidence as this and with the quiet atmosphere of the garden, one can picture that first Easter morning, the breathless hush as the women stole through the dawn, and their bewildered joy as they heard the angel's message: "He is risen. He is not here."

Not everyone has the wonderful opportunity of visiting the Holy Land, and even those who go to Jerusalem cannot always be certain that they have seen the exact spot where these wondrous events took place. But the angel's message is the same for us all. He is risen. Our Lord is not buried in some far-off land which we shall never see. He is alive for evermore, interceding for us at the throne of God, living through his Holy Spirit in the hearts of those who love him. He is not a dead Savior, but a living, loving, understanding friend.

A woman who knew the custodian of the garden tomb was given a cutting from one of the bushes of wormwood which border the paths there. A slip from this cutting took root on our return in the sunny garden of an old gray stone thatched cottage among the Dorset hills, a reminder of that other garden in which the power of death was conquered forever.

"The Garden Joy" was written by Irene, whose name means peace and who entered into the presence of her Savior not long after our pilgrimage.

> *The wagtail swings on the willow;*
> *The woodpecker laughs on the lawn;*
> *The goldfinch nests in the pear tree;*
> *Cuckoos call from the early dawn.*
> *Blue butterflies rest on the catmint;*
> *Round the lavender honeybees swarm;*
> *A squirrel peeps out from the pea-sticks;*
> *The strawberries are rosy and warm.*
>
> *But rarest of all in my borders*
> *Is the wormwood, silver and gray,*
> *A cutting from Calvary's garden*
> *In Jerusalem, far, far away.*
> *There in another fair garden,*
> *With white doves circling round,*
> *Mid bushes of silver-gray wormwood,*
> *The tomb of Christ Jesus was found.*
>
> *Pick what you will of my flowers,*
> *Share my bird song and sunshine and glee,*
> *But pray as you pass by the wormwood,*
> *For Christ died for you and for me.*

Mount Olivet

While there is doubt about some of the sacred sites, there can be none about the Mount of Olives or Olivet as it is called in the Acts. Olivet is a very distinctive feature of the landscape, a rounded gray hill lying to the east of Jerusalem and separated from the city by the deep valley of the Kedron.

The hillside is studded with churches, convents, and orphanages, and its grassy slopes are picturesque with dark pointed cypresses and gray-green olive trees. The Garden of Gethsemane lies just above the valley while high on the summit stands the Church of the Ascension with a group of other churches and a tall tower pointing heavenwards.

From our windows in the hotel we saw the Mount of Olives all golden in the dawn. We climbed it in shimmering heat at midday and stood on the tower to gaze down at Jerusalem seen in a windy sunset. Sometimes clouds gathered over the Mount, such clouds as once received the Lord out of mortal sight.

The Mount of Olives is surely the most highly honored of all the mountains of this world. Jesus loved to climb its slopes, to visit his friends in Bethany on the eastern side, the welcoming home of Lazarus and his sisters. He often spent time in the Garden of Gethsemane with his disciples, so that

Judas knew where the Lord would be on the night of betrayal. From Bethphage Jesus rode down the hill toward Jerusalem on Palm Sunday and was welcomed as the King coming in the name of the Lord. From Olivet he wept over the city which was to reject him. In the Garden on that hill he suffered agony for our sakes. And from the mountaintop he ascended victorious to his Father. One day it is promised that he will stand again on the Mount of Olives, this time in majesty and power.

The second coming of our Lord is sometimes ignored by Christians. Two thousand years have passed and the promised return is not yet. Two thousand years is a very short time in the history of the world. It may be very soon now, but we are warned not to fix a date for that great event, only to watch and be ready that we may be found faithful. It is a spur to urge us on, to keep us ever active in his service. What a glorious hope it is!

"This same Jesus, which is taken up from you into heaven, shall so come in like manner as ye have seen him go into heaven" (Acts 1:11).

And it is a hope not only for ourselves but for those we love in Christ, those who have gone before.

"The dead in Christ shall rise first: then we which are alive and remain shall be caught up together with them in the clouds, to meet the Lord in the air: and so shall we ever be with the Lord" (1 Thessalonians 4:17).

What is our job now? Making a home where Jesus is loved and welcomed as Martha, Mary, and Lazarus did on Olivet? Crowning him King in our lives as did the people who hailed him with palms as he rode by? (Those who greeted him thus were probably followers from Galilee who camped on Olivet during the crowded festival seasons. They were not the rabble who yelled for Barabbas.) Is the part God has given us the way of suffering? Then let us bear his will as Jesus did in Gethsemane, learning obedience and patience in our agony. Perhaps for us there is that simple command, so hard to obey: Watch and pray.

The Hill Country

"And Mary arose in those days, and went into the hill country with haste, into a city of Juda; and entered into the house of Zacharias, and saluted Elisabeth."

Ein Karim is the name today of that city of Juda. It is a small village, a few miles from Jerusalem. Houses, packed tightly together, straggle up a steep hill on both sides of a street so narrow that there is only space enough for a thin donkey to pass along. A fat one would soon get stuck, as donkeys are generally well loaded. Dark-eyed children in gay colored clothes peep at the strangers from arched doorways. Young mothers with babies in their arms watch with curiosity from slits of windows. Old women gossip and nod by their gateways. At the foot of the hill the main road from Jerusalem is busy with traffic, cars, coaches, and trucks. An ice-cream kiosk at the corner offers modern wares for sale: cool drinks, cosmetics, camera films, and cheap toys for people who look as if they had stepped out of the pages of an illustrated Old Testament.

On the far side of the main road a lane winds up another hill. Wild flowers grow in profusion on its banks and the children of Ein Karim gather bunches to sell. This way leads to a church built to commemorate the meeting of the mother

67

of our Lord with her cousin Elisabeth. A great plaque covering a long wall down one side of the rose garden gives the words of the Magnificat, the hymn of Mary in almost all the languages of the world.

We must not worship Mary, nor give to her the honor due to Christ, the Holy Son of God, but we reverence her as the mother of our Lord, remembering the words of the angel Gabriel: "Hail, thou that art highly favoured, the Lord is with thee: blessed art thou among women."

The words Mary spoke when she met Elisabeth have been used as a hymn by the Christian church, a hymn of praise to God for the honor he had bestowed upon a simple village maiden. There is no sign of fear, no anxiety about her own reputation, no hesitation as to whether she had acted wisely. Mary trusted God absolutely and had only thanksgiving in her heart because he who had never failed his people had chosen her to serve him.

Notice how Mary recalls God's goodness in the past. She does not forget the story of her nation and God's mercy shown from generation to generation. Do we think enough about our own country and do we pray for God's guidance to our leaders?

Mary must have known that she would have to face misunderstanding, but she does not worry about difficulties. God to her is a living reality. See how she uses the words *me* and *my*:

"God my Savior." [He] "hath done unto me great things."

"My soul doth magnify the Lord." "My spirit hath rejoiced."

She trusted her own life to God. Because she knew his ways and his dealings with his people of old, she could confidently pass on to us the promise: "His mercy is on them that fear him from generation to generation."

Can we trust him with our future, our health, our reputation? He is just the same today.

Road to Bethlehem

We did not take the traditional route of the Wise Men when we went from Jerusalem to Bethlehem. We traveled in modern taxis, but we thought of the Magi following the star, especially when we were stopped by a strange convoy coming towards us—a caravan of four stately camels ridden by four handsomely clad Arabs. East met West and the road was narrow, giving no room to pass; so West yielded and the camels plodded on their way, a supercilious sneer on their aristocratic faces. Their riders greeted us with dignified courtesy. Such a sight is infrequent in the very up-to-date state of Israel. Camels are becoming rare as means of transport now.

It was a lonely road among the hills. The taxis drove at speed round sharp hairpin bends and along the verge of steep precipices. Range upon range of rust-red mountains stretched away into the distance, the highlands of Judea. Beyond in the east lay the blue mountains of Moab. On the sun-baked, wind-swept slopes by the roadside every patch of green grass fed some flock of long-eared sheep or skinny, agile black goats. Beneath a mulberry tree a ring of little girls danced, singing a wailing song. Though villages were few, there were plenty of people about, for the hills were riddled with caves, very useful as free homes. They looked from the road like dark slits in the rocks but our guide said they were quite roomy inside.

David, the shepherd boy of Bethlehem, must often have climbed these hills and gone exploring among the caves. He knew where to hide when he had to flee from Saul, and he was accustomed to cave life from his boyhood. He understood the troubles of the homeless, so he made a home for the distressed in the Cave Adullam.

David's greater Son understood even better the suffering of the homeless, those in debt and the bitter of soul. Jesus himself was a refugee. At his birth there was no room for him in the inn. Born in a stable, his cradle was a borrowed manger. In infancy, he had to be taken into exile in Egypt. Later his home town rejected him. His triumphal ride was on a borrowed donkey. He ate the last Passover in a borrowed room. Condemned to a criminal's death, his body was laid in a borrowed tomb.

Yes, he understands about the needs of the distressed. There is one way in which we can serve him and that is by helping them. The world today is crowded with the homeless, the famine-stricken, the sick, and the despairing. Anything we can do for them is doing it for Jesus. "Inasmuch as ye have done it unto one of the least of these my brethren, ye have done it unto me" (Matt. 25:40). Is there any way you can work for others—by gifts if you have money, by helping some society for the relief of war victims, orphans or wounded? If you can do nothing else, you can pray, and perhaps that is the greatest need of all.

Silver Star

Everybody must have seen Bethlehem at some time, either on television or in illustrated books or on calendars and Christmas cards. The scene is so well known that approaching Bethlehem is like returning to a well-loved home town. The hill crowded with white houses and church towers, the sound of the bell of the Church of the Nativity so often heard on records or on the radio, all are so familiar. The many sight-seers, cameras flashing and ready with "backsheesh" for anyone in Arab clothing who is willing to pose for a photo-graph, are to be expected in so famous a town. The busy courtyard of the Church of the Nativity was thronged with pilgrims when we arrived, and yes, there it was, the little door we had always heard of, so low that the most important man on earth must bow his head when he enters the place where Jesus was born.

The church is built on the place where the inn once stood. Justin, writing less than 150 years after the birth of Christ, mentioned that Jesus was born in a cave near Bethlehem. The church, and the old inn or khan which it replaced, is near the city and the grotto is certainly a cave, probably the far end of the stable which would be large enough to hold camels as well as asses or mules.

Bethlehem must have been just as crowded that night when Joseph came up from Galilee to the city of David. People sometimes wonder why he should have taken Mary with him at such a time. Luke, always an accurate historian, gives us the reason. The census ordered by the Roman Emperor, Caesar Augustus, for purposes of taxation made it necessary for every man to go to his own city and Joseph was a native of Bethlehem and belonged to the house of David. Joseph, warned by the angel, knew that the child to be born was the long-promised Messiah. He must have seen in this Roman order the hand of God fulfilling the prophecy of Micah 5:2.

"Thou, Bethlehem Ephratah, though thou be little among the thousands of Judah, yet out of thee shall he come forth unto me that is to be ruler in Israel."

The child of Mary must be born in Bethlehem, and so it happened without any carefully contrived plan of action. The Romans knew nothing of Micah and his prophecies but in God's hand is the whole world. Augustus and Cyrenius did his will without knowing it. If every man was to go to his own town to be taxed, Joseph had no alternative but to take Mary with him.

The taxation brought problems to little Bethlehem—one inn and crowds coming from every part of the Roman Empire. All available lodging space was filled. When Joseph came with Mary in her hour of need there was only the small cave at the end of the stable yard to offer them. What would that innkeeper say if he came to Bethlehem today and saw thousands coming from every quarter of the globe to worship the child who was born that busy night in the stable?

The Church of the Nativity is dark and somber, lit by red lamps glowing with crystal balls like Christmas tree decorations. Priests of the Greek Orthodox Church move silently about and there is a strange scent of incense. The walls are covered with beautiful mosaics. Each marble column is made of a single stone.

The grotto of the Nativity lies about twenty feet below the floor of the choir. Fifteen silver lamps burn perpetually above a plain silver star on the floor which shows where Jesus was born.

The embroidered hangings, the jewels, the ornaments, the mosaics, the rather gaudy decorations, the smell of the incense, all these pass from our minds as we kneel for a moment to thank God for his great gift to mankind. Only a moment is allowed for each pilgrim. Long lines of men, women, and children from many nations are waiting for their turn to pray, to kneel and kiss the silver star. Then out of the dark church we pass into the glad sunlight where the bells of Bethlehem are ringing.

There is no sign now of the lowly cattle shed. Our Lord is no longer an infant for whom the inn had no room. He is King of Kings and Lord of Lords and we are proud to be called his servants.

Isn't it glorious to realize that this great eternal King has lived our life, from helpless infancy to full manhood. He knows and understands all our needs and anxieties. He was in all points tempted like as we are, yet without sin.

"Good tidings of great joy which shall be to all people."

Shepherds' Field

A reading from the Old Testament today and whatever has this strange story to do with the story of Bethlehem?

Jesus loved the Old Testament which he learned as a boy. He quoted most frequently from the Book of Deuteronomy. The story of Balaam is important in the history of the children of Israel and it has a message for us, too.

About a mile from Bethlehem and within sight of the city is the place known as "The Shepherds' Field." It is enclosed by rough stone walls, a sloping grassy field with a cave in the middle where shepherds could shelter their flocks in bad weather. Grass is scarce in the Holy Land and, since there are few streams for watering sheep, the flocks have to be constantly moved to find fresh pasture. The work of shepherds is often mentioned in the Bible and the best loved story of all is that of the shepherds who saw the angels in the field near Bethlehem.

We saw no angels there and no sheep or shepherds. All we found was scanty sun-dried grass, a few pine cones from two or three thin trees and three donkeys, one a little white foal and his nervous gray mother. The third was a brown ass staggering down the lane under the weight of such a tremendous haystack that the poor beast was almost invisible.

If shepherds appear frequently in the Bible records, donkeys too make a good showing. There was the colt, the foal of an ass, upon which Jesus rode on Palm Sunday; the ass which Abraham took with Isaac and the servants to make sacrifice of his son; the asses lost by Saul's father; the dead ass whose jawbone Samson used to kill a thousand of the Philistines. It would be interesting to study the message God sends through all these asses. Balaam's ass has a word for us today. Like the shepherds of Bethlehem, Balaam's ass saw an angel.

It is a very human predicament, to know what is right and yet to do wrong. Balak, king of Moab, tried to bribe Balaam the seer to make him curse the children of Israel. At first Balaam staunchly refused. He knew the Israelites were God's people. But the king and his bribes were tempting. Balaam began to waver. He did not wish to sin, but he did not wish to anger the king. With his mind in a state of compromise, he saddled his ass and set off to soon find himself in a most unpleasant position. There he was in a narrow path between vineyards with a wall on each side. His ass was bucking and jibbing beneath him, bumping her rider against the stone walls.

Haven't you often felt like that when yielding to temptation? To sin does not always bring satisfaction, generally it means bitter remorse. Balaam might have stood out courageously and gone down in history as one of the great prophets of the Lord. Instead he prophesied only under compulsion. God put the words in his mouth and it was a great prophecy, but it was not given willingly. God does speak sometimes through unworthy lips, for all men are known to him and can be used to fulfill his purpose.

The ass had more sense than Balaam. She saw the angel standing in the way with a drawn sword in his hand. Balaam saw nothing until the ass spoke.

We do not see angels now, but we have been given conscience. Those who are Christ's must give heed to the least temptation. Sin has awful consequences.

Down to Jericho

One of the delights of traveling in the Holy Land is the continual discovery of how accurate the Bible is. Jericho is an illustration of this point.

The Old Testament story in the Book of Joshua describes it as a walled city raised above the surrounding country, so that when the walls fell flat, "the people shall ascend up every man straight before him" (6:5). The New Testament story speaks of going "down from Jerusalem to Jericho" (Luke 10:30). Yet both are right. It depends on which way you are going.

The ruins of the ancient city form a tremendous mound which has been excavated by archaeologists. They discovered a succession of cities, built, destroyed, and built again on the same spot, a strategic place for defense, a hill in the middle of a plain, well supplied with water. Joshua and his men coming from the east across Jordan would have to ascend to the city, but the man who fell among thieves did not come that way. He was journeying from Jerusalem.

Jesus spoke from personal knowledge of the country. He himself had traveled that way, and the story of the Good Samaritan was founded on fact.

"A certain man went down from Jerusalem to Jericho." The road from Jerusalem passes over the Mount of Olives and then winds steeply downhill. It is a formidable descent, sweeping round sharp corners, lonely and wild in the rugged grandeur of red-tinged mountains. Great outcropings of rock would make excellent lurking places for robbers. Even today, though the road surface has been improved for motorized traffic, it is hardly safe to travel there alone. From the top of the Olivet range the road goes down until it reaches the lowest point on the surface of the earth, the Plain of the Dead Sea which lies there, deep blue and tranquil in a desolation of salt. The air grows hotter and hotter as one descends. The breeze is like hot breath.

Modern Jericho is a pleasant little village not far from the ruins of the old city. It is well watered and vegetation is lush with grass among the pools. Jericho was called "the city of palm trees." Date palms, apples, and bananas all grow there. The heat is exhausting, but electric fans cool the air for the luxurious villas of the wealthy. The Lido on the Dead Sea provides bathing and amusements, entertainment for dwellers in one of the oldest cities on earth, inhabited continuously for at least nine thousand years.

The Jordan, which the children of Israel crossed on their way to Jericho, is bordered by thickets of tamarisk and willows, but as the river approaches the Dead Sea, plant life fails, leaving only the sad saltwort and the apples of Sodom. Piles of salt stand stark and white, reminding one of Lot's wife who looked back to the luxury and sin of the cities of the plain and became herself a pillar of salt. The fresh water of the river pours into the sea from which there is no outlet. In the depths of that great hollow evaporation is intense and salt destroys all life. The water is too salty to drink. Fish cannot live in it. After bathing there one must wash away the salt in fresh water to save one's skin.

Yet throughout the ages, God had his hidden treasures in that lifeless water. Natural gas and mineral deposits are now being developed and will be a most valuable asset for the economy of Israel and Jordan. The desolate, rocky country on the shores of the Dead Sea, too, in recent years has yielded up treasures of great value. The discoveries in the caves of Qumran include many portions of the Old Testament, one of which is a manuscript of Isaiah older than the oldest Hebrew versions and wonderfully preserved in the arid atmosphere of the deep gorge.

Going down to Jericho is dangerous (especially nowadays if one's brakes are not sound), but the climb up to Jerusalem is a real test of endurance. The terrific heat and the long slow climb are agonizing when taken on foot. There is another route which Jesus could have chosen when journeying to Jerusalem. He could have avoided Jericho. He was on the way to the cross. Why choose that difficult and dangerous road?

Jericho was not only the charming city of palm trees. It was an accursed city. The Israelites were commanded to destroy it utterly and never to rebuild it. But it was rebuilt by Hiel the Bethelite, who sacrificed his eldest son to bury in the foundations and his youngest beneath the gates. Jericho, the city of sin, needed a Savior and Jesus came to seek and to save that which was lost. It was the last journey of his earthly life and two souls were in desperate need, blind Bartimaeus at the entering in and Zacchaeus, the little publican, on the far side. All the people of Jericho saw the miracle and heard the words of forgiveness and had one more chance to repent and believe.

Hidden treasure in the Dead Sea, hidden treasure in the lonely rock caves, Jesus sees hidden treasure of greater value in the souls of men. The man who went downhill fell among thieves. Jesus went on purpose through the city of sin as he journeyed towards the cross.

"And all the people, when they saw it, gave praise unto God."

House of God

"That is Bethel over there," said David our guide, pointing to a flat waste ground scattered with large stones.

Bethel, the House of God, the place where young Jacob lay down for the night, a miserable exile from his home, depressed by memories of his own mean behavior in the past and uncertainty about his prospects in the future. What a hard stony bed to lie on! To be sure we could see one large white stone shaped like a pillow in a neat pillowcase, but there was no down or feathers to soothe Jacob's weary head. Footsore, unhappy, and ashamed, he piled up stones to lie on and tried to forget his misery in sleep.

God, who knows all our troubles, sent something better than sleep. In his dreams Jacob saw a ladder set up on the earth and reaching up to heaven. Upon it the angels of God were ascending and descending, and the Lord stood above it with the promise: "Behold, I am with thee and will keep thee in all places whither thou goest, and will bring thee again into this land."

Over and over again God has promised to be with his people.

"Even to your old age I am he; and even to hoar hairs will I carry you" (Isa. 46:4).

"Fear thou not; for I am with thee: be not dismayed; for I am thy God: I will strengthen thee; yea, I will help thee; yea I will uphold thee with the right hand of my righteousness" (Isa. 41:10).

"I will never leave thee, nor forsake thee" (Heb. 13:5).

"Lo, I am with you alway, even unto the end of the world" (Matt. 28:20).

So, if you have a hard bed to lie on tonight—a bed of sorrow, or of bitter remorse with a pillow of sad memories and anxious fears—if the future holds only uncertainty and the present is full of care, then remember Jacob at Bethel and what God said to him there.

Twenty years later, Jacob returned to Bethel. There he renewed his vows and God gave him a new name. He was to be no longer Jacob the Deceiver, but henceforth he was to be called Israel the Prince. A new name and a new nature, wonderful gifts from God. Jacob was not promised a life free from sorrow. Even there at Bethel bereavement came. As he journeyed on his way, Rachel his beloved wife died. Suffering is common to all men, and serving God is no insurance policy against pain. But when we know God's love we are given strength to bear whatever may come.

Our verse from the Revelation is not connected with the story of Jacob, but it holds a message for every Christian. God knows our weaknesses. He knows how to change them to his glory. In the mystic white stone he has a special name for each one, a name of victory over some temptation, a name of hope or of comfort. It is a secret name known only to you and to God.

Day 27—1 Samuel 9:1-20; Genesis 31:43-50

Mizpeh

Israel's communal farms are extremely modern and well run, but there are still parts of the country where the life of the Old Testament remains as simple and primitive as ever. Between Jerusalem and Samaria you can see men harvesting with sickles and women sitting on the ground to bind the sheaves. Oxen tread out the corn by tramping round and round the threshing floors. Camels lurch through a field of onions. A graceful young girl walks down to the well with an earthenware pitcher balanced on her head, and her mother follows carrying a baby on her hip. Little boys, brown as berries, toil in vineyards and strawberry plantations. A mule and an ox struggle along together beneath an uneven yoke. All along the roadside trail masses of convulvulus, a deep, royal blue.

The Hill Mizpeh, like a pointed watchtower on the horizon, locates the picture in our reading today. This was the home country of Kish of the tribe of Benjamin, the father of Saul, the first king of Israel. The old man by a gate saying good-bye to a bronzed youth with a donkey, might well have been the prophet Samuel talking to Saul, the chosen king.

Saul was a choice young man and goodly. Tall and well-built, he had the advantage of having been brought up in the open-air life of a farmer's son. He was well equipped in physical strength. As a youth he was not proud and did not seek any high position for himself. He was brave and a great warrior, necessary in those warlike days. Best of all, the Spirit of God came upon him.

He began so well, yet at the end of his life Saul was a failure and died the death of a coward on the field of battle.

"The shield of the mighty is vilely cast away, the shield of Saul, as though he had not been anointed with oil" (2 Sam. 1:21).

The anointed king had failed in his duty to God. Self-will, pride, jealousy, and disobedience, allowed to dwell in his heart, gradually overcame the high hopes and aspirations of his youth.

There is another Mizpeh in our second reading. It is sometimes spelled *Mizpah* and the word means "a watchtower." This was the Mizpah in Gilead where Laban and Jacob built a pile of stones before they parted. In Victorian days it was the custom for friends to give one another a Mizpah ring, plain gold inscribed with the word Mizpah, meaning "The Lord watch between me and thee while we are absent one from another." The Bible story, however, does not give these words as a token of faithful love. On the contrary, Laban was highly suspicious of his son-in-law. He was a cheat himself, and he knew Jacob to be a deceiver. The message of Mizpah was a warning to Jacob not to ill-treat his two wives, the daughters of Laban.

Mizpeh of Benjamin reminds us that even the most promising beginning may end in failure. Mizpah of Gilead reminds us also that God sees the inner thoughts which are the beginning of sin.

Wealth in Samaria

It was the hottest part of a scorching day when we entered Samaria, now known by the less interesting name of Sebaste. We were too tired to go any farther. Not for us was the weary climb over rocks and ruins to see the remains of Ahab's ivory palace, the great stairway of the temple built by Herod, the Avenue of Columns, or the Roman Gateway.

Some energetic enthusiasts pushed on but we sat down by a small shop and drank pink lemonade in a garden filled with red lilies and hollyhocks. Hollyhocks, typical of English gardens and of gardens in the New World, too, all had their ancestry in the Holy Land, for it was the Crusaders who brought home big dry seed pods and introduced to their cottage gardens the tall, flaunting spires of color, calling them "Holy Hocks," which became "Hollyhocks."

Camels plodded solemnly by us as we waited there. Veiled women came over the hill with their pitchers on their heads, balanced sideways if empty but upright on their return from the well. Bright-eyed boys running home from school paused to stare at the waiting strangers and tried to sell us old Roman coins and American chewing gum.

The four men in our story waited outside Samaria once long ago, four wretched, starving lepers, hopeless and de-

85

spairing. Nobody wanted them. The city was under siege and food supplies there were exhausted after weeks of famine. If they went into Sàmaria, they would starve. If they sat still where they were, they would die of hunger or be killed by the Syrians encamped all round.

Fear of the besieging army was not so intense as the horror of starvation and possible cannibalism. They decided to face the camp of the Syrians, saying: "If they save us alive, we shall live; and if they kill us, we shall but die."

So terrified, they crept through the twilight towards the tents of the enemy. And, behold, there was no man there! The whole army had vanished, and in the enemy camp there was food enough for the starving besieged city, besides gold, silver, and raiment.

How many of our fears are groundless! How many international problems could be solved if the nations of the world could share the good things God has provided. In material things, there are bountiful supplies, enough for all, if selfishness could be conquered and all would share.

And in spiritual matters too, inexhaustible supplies of God's grace are waiting to be appropriated by those who hunger and thirst after righteousness. "They shall be filled" is the Lord's promise. Do we need more love in our hearts, more courage to face the future, more perseverance, more faith, hope, purity, a deeper devotion, a richer filling of the Holy Spirit? God has all this to give, life more abundant for you. There is no need to linger, afraid of an enemy who has already been conquered for you. There is no need to fear starvation of soul when Jesus has promised: "I am the bread of life: he that cometh to me shall never hunger; and he that believeth on me shall never thirst" (John 6:35).

City of Refuge

It was in Shechem that God spoke to Abraham when he first came to Canaan and there the promise was given: "Unto thy seed will I give this land" (Gen. 12:7).

When the children of Israel entered the Promised Land after the captivity in Egypt, Shechem was appointed as one of the six cities of refuge to which any man who had killed another without intention to murder might find safety.

Shechem was the capital of the country in the time of Solomon and here, Solomon's son, Rehoboam, made the fatal decision which lost him half his kingdom. So the town of Shechem is very old and full of history.

You would not expect that if you traveled through casually, for today Shechem is a beautiful place on the slopes between Mount Gerizim, the Mount of Blessing and Mount Ebal, the Mount of Cursing. Its comfortable white houses all possess cool verandas, shaded by flowering trees, the blue-belled jacaranda, the scarlet hibiscus, and the ever-present oleander brilliant with purple and pink. But all who live in Shechem are not wealthy.

We went to Shechem on purpose to meet the last surviving members of the race of Samaritans. There are very few of them left now and they cling together tenaciously, struggling

87

to maintain their small community in spite of great poverty. Descended from the mixed race which peopled that part of the country after the Assyrians killed or took prisoner all the men of the Northern Kingdom, they were never really integrated with the Jews and there was open hostility in New Testament times as we read in the Gospels. Now they are looked upon as a curious survival of the past, in fact they are an advantage to the tourist industry of Israel on account of their strange customs.

The Samaritans keep the Law of Moses strictly and are particular about the observance of the Sabbath Day. They do not follow all the Jewish law, with its teaching of rabbinical tradition. The Samaritans obey only that which is contained in the first five books of the Bible. Their greatest treasure is an ancient manuscript of these books, "the Samaritan Codex." A tall, black-bearded priest escorted us around the Samaritan synogogue and showed us the Codex with great pride. He told us that their center of worship is still as of old on Mount Gerizim, not in Jerusalem. They were refused admittance to the temple at Jerusalem when they were first introduced into the country after the Captivity, so they set up their own temple among whose ruins their descendants still make the sacrifice of a lamb at the Passover.

"Our fathers worshiped in this mountain," said the Samaritan woman at the well to Jesus, "and ye say, that in Jerusalem is the place where men ought to worship."

"The hour cometh," replied Jesus, "when ye shall neither in this mountain, nor yet at Jerusalem, worship the Father. . . . God is a Spirit: and they that worship him must worship him in spirit and in truth."

The well, where those wonderful words were spoken is outside the city and it is one of the sites in the Holy Land about which there is no doubt. There is plenty of water flowing in the district, but only one well, the well which Jacob dug in order to keep himself and his family separate from the idolators of Shechem. A church has been built over it, but the well is the most honored part of the building.

"The well is deep," said the woman to Jesus. Her words are true. One of our party read aloud the story and when he came to those words he paused. The priest in charge of the church took a can of water and poured it down. Several moments passed before the sound of the splash was heard. Then he drew water up from the well for us to drink, and we knew that we should indeed thirst again, for the day was very hot. The water of Jacob's well was but earthly refreshment. Jesus promises us, as he promised to that woman, living water, a well of water springing up into everlasting life.

"Your Jesus did not despise us Samaritans," said the priest at the synagogue. "Your Jesus told the story of the Good Samaritan and he noticed that among the ten lepers who were healed the only grateful one was a Samaritan. He spoke kindly to the woman at the well, although she was a Samaritan. Your Jesus loved us Samaritans."

Yes, and he loves the Samaritans still, those earnest few who live in the City of Refuge and have not yet found the true refuge from sin. They sacrifice a lamb at the Passover, but they do not come to the Lamb of God which taketh away the sin of the world. Here is a bit of missionary work for you today. Will you pray that the remaining Samaritans may learn to say not, "Your Jesus," but "Our Jesus." Pray that those who live so near to Jacob's well may drink of the Living Water offered freely to all.

View from Pisgah

By the last day, most of us had spent all our money. Some wished to spend the remaining hours quietly before beginning the journey home; others felt no particular interest in seeing the Roman ruins at Jerash in Jordan. That trip however included climbing Mount Nebo to the spur known as Pisgah.

When Moses came to the borders of the Promised Land on the east of the Dead Sea, God showed him that view.

"Get thee up into the top of Pisgah, and lift up thine eyes westward, and northward, and southward, and eastward, and behold it with thine eyes: for thou shalt not go over this Jordan" (Deut. 3:27).

The view which Moses looked upon is like a relief map of the whole country. Four thousand feet below lies the Dead Sea, like a placid sheet of blue glass. The Jordan valley, vivid in green fertility, winds snakelike down to the Dead Sea between ranges of bare hills. From the rusty mountains beyond Hebron in the South to the green hills of Galilee in the North, there stretches all this little precious land of Canaan, the earthly homeland of the Son of God. West of the Dead Sea is Jericho, the city of palm trees. Farther south is Bethlehem. Encircled by mountains, yet raised above them, Jerusalem stands on her majestic heights. In the rich plains of Samaria

91

Mount Ebal and Mount Gerizim are clearly visible, and beyond them the enormous rounded bulk of the solitary Mount Tabor. A distant streak of blue shows the Sea of Galilee and some hundred and twenty miles away the snowy summit of Mount Hermon gleams.

The dim eyes of the aged leader must have glimpsed this fair country spread out before him, and he must have ached with longing to reach the land for which he had spent so many years wandering in the wilderness. But not for him was the entering in. He could only view the landscape and then turn sadly away. Others were to cross the Jordan, to conquer Jericho and march on to possess the land. For Moses there was only an unknown grave on a lonely hill.

God had prepared something better for his faithful servant. In his lifetime Moses saw the Promised Land from afar. Centuries after his death Moses entered in.

Was snow-capped Hermon the mountain chosen to be the scene of the Transfiguration? I do not think that Moses even noticed the stately hills, the rich plains, the populous towns or the sacred sites revered by his race throughout the centuries. On the Mount of Transfiguration Moses and Elijah stood with Jesus the Christ, which is far better.

We may be in America, in Europe, in Asia, in Australia, in Africa or in Antarctica. We do not need to go to Palestine to be with Jesus now. He is with every believer and that is all that matters. Where Jesus is, that is hallowed ground.

The journey of life for a Christian is a pilgrimage to a Promised Land, far better than Canaan. It is a joyous journey, for we do not travel alone. On the way there are both joys and sorrows to encounter and there is much to look forward to.

"Eye hath not seen, nor ear heard, neither have entered into the heart of man, the things which God hath prepared for them that love him" (1 Cor. 2:9).

Dark waters separate us from those eternal joys, the deep valley of the Jordan, the river of death, but we need not fear the depths or the darkness, for we shall not pass over alone. "I will fear no evil, for Thou art with me."

Then, the pilgrimage completed: "Thine eyes shall see the king in his beauty: they shall behold the land that is very far off" (Isa. 33:17).